# How to Discover Your Child's Unique Gifts

# RALPH MATTSON

LIFEJOURNEY
BOOKS

LifeJourney Books is an imprint of David C. Cook
Publishing Co.
David C. Cook Publishing Co., Elgin, Illinois 60120
David C. Cook Publishing Co., Weston, Ontario
Nova Distribution, Ltd., Torquay, England

How to Discover Your Child's Gifts
©1991 by Ralph Mattson
(This booklet consists of selected portions of *Discovering
Your Child's Design* ©1989 by Ralph Mattson and Thom
Black)

Edited by Brian Reck
Cover design by Bob Fuller
First printing, 1991
Printed in the United States of America
95 94 93 92 91  5 4 3 2 1

**Library of Congress Cataloging in Publication Data**
Mattson, Ralph
How to Discover Your Child's Gifts/ Ralph Mattson
    p.  cm. — (Helping Families Grow series)
ISBN: 1-55513-697-4
1. Child development. 2. Child psychology. 3. Personality
development. 4. Diaries—Authorship.    I. Mattson, Ralph
II. Title. III. Series
HQ772.M378   1991
155.4—dc20                                      91-27569
                                                CIP

Parents are in a highly strategic position when it comes to gathering evidence for their child's design. No one else has the opportunity to observe the child's actions in so many conditions and situations. Yet parents play a supervisory role so often that they occasionally fail to see all the drama taking place about them.

Even when doing ordinary things, a person's actions express something of the unique individual he or she happens to be. Merely walking down the hall displays a distinctive expression.

How much more revealing are the

complex activities of play and school when discovering a child's design. Careful observation of these activities will reveal splendid consistencies. To aid in the process, it is helpful to keep a Design Journal.

## BEGINNING A DESIGN JOURNAL

As you start to keep your Design Journal, you will soon discover that it will help you record several valuable pieces of information.

1. *Record the action.* A primary purpose of your journal is to record your child's actions. This is where you imagine yourself as an objective reporter gathering only facts. At this early stage you should be totally disinterested in anybody's opinion about those facts, including your own. All you want to include in this section of the Design Journal are notes describing specific actions. You need only make a record of them, taking notes on both primary and secondary actions.

Primary actions include specific accomplishments. For example: a building of blocks was put together, a jigsaw puzzle was assembled, a bath drain was unplugged, a drawing was completed, a tricycle or bicycle was ridden for the first time, a school project was finished, a toy battle was fought, seeds were planted, bread was baked, a room was organized, a club was established, a collection was assembled, a playpen was outgrown, costumes were made, scrapbooks were put together, races were run, picnics were organized, etc.

Secondary actions are the activities that either precede or follow the primary actions. For instance: all the necessary tools were gathered, someone was persuaded to join the team, a mess was cleaned up, directions were read and followed, shapes were analyzed, materials were located and assembled, practice took place, something was designed on paper, a procedure was learned, information was obtained, words were mastered, skills were learned, a team was formed, an animal was trained, paint was applied, ingredients were weighed, a process was controlled, a script was followed, a fantasy was created, a list was made, and so forth.

2. *Record significant quotes from your observation.* As your child is involved in his or her activities, you will overhear a running commentary. The second function of

the Design Journal is to record useful quotes, such as: "It's more fun when Bobby plays with me;" "I like drawings that are hard to do;" "My tower is higher than yours;" "Do it like the picture says;" "Let me change it;" "There are too many pieces;" "I like math;" "Now let me tell you a scary story;" "Can I help you make the cookies?" "Show me how;" "I'm the teacher;" "Let's do a different one;" "I hate baseball;" "Do it right!" or "Let's see where we end up."

3. *Record significant quotes gleaned from the child's story telling.* You may not happen to overhear enough to let you know clearly what the child is thinking or feeling. So as you question him a bit, record his responses in this third section of the Design Journal. This process is described in detail later in this booklet.

4. *Record your preliminary ideas about what you see.* As you gather and record observations, you will start to see the emergence of certain themes or consistencies. You might discover that your child doesn't like to make a move until he knows exactly what is expected, likes to organize his room and his toys even when they don't need it, likes to do things with others, likes

to write stories, doesn't like to read instructions, or so forth. You should write down these consistencies whether they are fully proven facts or mere suspicions. As they accumulate in your Design Journal, they become a major resource for reaching some clear conclusions about your child.

## LEARNING TO ACCEPT WHAT GOD HAS DONE

Having worked with many parents over the years, I see a too common tendency among many of them. Some encourage only the behavior of their children that reinforces the parent's personal desires for the child. And even worse, other parents firmly insist that a child shape himself into the model the parent has created. No words can express the deep sadness and even bitterness that children develop when a parent fails to appreciate what the child really is.

Classic stories abound of the results of this tragic parental stubbornness. A mother gives thousands of signals that she wanted a daughter instead of a son, creating life-long confusion for that son. A father wants his son to be the athlete he never was, and the child has no choice in the matter. A parent demands more and more from a child until the only standard the child knows is perfection.

Both the misdirected athlete and the unrelenting perfectionist may go to their graves never enjoying the satisfaction of a job well done. They simply never learned how. And as these people become parents, the problem is perpetuated with their own children.

So you think that all normal people love to be on teams, but your child doesn't even seem to know what a team is? Write down the evidence and debate with God later. Your daughter is an expert reader but doesn't display the love of books you had at her age? Don't worry about it—just record the facts. Your son is a great football player but doesn't have the "killer instinct" you hoped he would develop? Your accounting skills taught your child to complete any math problem, but she just doesn't enjoy it like you do? You're trying to teach meekness, and your son wants to be a combination of Rambo and G.I. Joe? Your little girl disregards your seamstress abilities in favor of shopping for her own clothes?

In each of these cases, you should be

patient. The best thing for everybody concerned is for you to accept what God has already done. Acknowledge His wisdom with gratitude. And set your child free to enjoy being the creature God intended him or her to be.

We do not make the assumption that all your child's behavior will be good, true, and beautiful. We know that the human race is desperately flawed and that those shortcomings show up early in life. But Scripture teaches that God gives good gifts to men whether they are saints or sinners. It is the identification and description of those gifts that you are after in the Design Journal. The overwhelming number of notes will provide supporting evidence for those gifts. The remaining notes will be merely chaff among the kernels, and can be ignored.

Keeping a Design Journal is rather simple. You don't need to note that your child serves himself some food, but you do record that he always takes a lot of time to arrange the food on his plate. You don't need to say that your child is responsible for filling the water glasses each night for the dinner table. But you would want to notice if she always makes sure the glasses have no spots, are lined up on a tray with exactly three ice cubes in each glass, and contain exactly the same level of water.

Pay attention to actions in which your child chooses to engage. We all need to serve ourselves food, but not everyone is concerned about how it is arranged on the plate. We may be required to fill the water glasses, but not to be precise about it.

## CHOICE OPPORTUNITIES

Whenever your child has an opportunity to make a choice, look for especially useful data. Perhaps she always heads toward the sandbox rather than the swings. He prefers blocks and building toys to tanks, trucks, and cars. She lines up her dolls to play nursery school rather than dressing or feeding them. He always likes to surprise you from behind the door or the couch rather than to simply run into your arms. She would rather bang on pots and pans than listen to a recording of children's songs. He chooses to draw pictures rather than play with dinosaurs. She would rather put together model airplanes than make cakes. He would rather save money than collect baseball cards.

When you take notes regarding these tendencies, you can't yet determine their significance. You don't need to analyze them yet. All you need do is collect them. But if they add up with other items, you may establish a preliminary pattern and then seek other evidence to confirm or disprove its existence.

The Design Journal becomes a workbook that leads you into understanding your child's design. The greater the detail you provide, the greater the possibility of accuracy in determining your child's design.

The Design Journal is different than most of the baby books you may be familiar with. Many parents have gone through a "baby book period" during the beginning months of their child's life. They attempt to record when baby first rolls over, when the first step takes place, the emergence of the first tooth, and so on.

The baby book concept is a good one in that it celebrates the miracle of development and focuses attention on the fierce progress of a growing child. But most parents are so busy caring for the child that they let the baby book slide. It is rare to see such a volume that doesn't start with detailed notes in the first pages and gradually decline into a mass of blank pages.

When subsequent children review the family archives, they ask why the oldest child has a baby book and they don't. The answer is, of course, that Mom and Dad quickly became realists. They realized that the magic of the first step holds much appeal when it first occurs, but beyond that point there are many other developments that dwarf its importance.

A Design Journal is a far more useful documentation of your child's life than the traditional baby books. When your child reaches adulthood, it will be fascinating for him to see exactly what path he took to get to where he is. The Design Journal provides a solid foundation for continued work in the identification and stewardship of giftedness in careers, ministry, service to others, marriage, and family life. What an extraordinary historical gift that will be!

## YOUR CHILD AS STORYTELLER

People have a natural inclination to share their feelings with another concerned person unless they have a good reason not to. When friends get together they swiftly move past the small talk and begin to discuss the matters that are really on their minds. And when you encourage children to let you know what they think about certain things, they are probably going to be quick to tell you—as long as they sense that you are genuinely concerned with what they have to say.

It is usually possible to discover the design of an individual by having him talk about his interests. If you want to confirm some observations you have made regarding your son or daughter, you can do so with informal discussion about events you have witnessed. And your child will probably add to your pool of information by telling stories about certain events which you haven't even observed yet.

## ENCOURAGE YOUR CHILDREN TO TELL STORIES

It is important to get your child's perspective on your observations, even if you have reached a conclusion that makes perfect sense to you. If six adults attend the same meeting, they are likely to emerge with six different stories about what actually took place during the meeting. Even with written minutes of the meeting, it is likely that each person would have a different interpretation about what they meant. The differences in opinion would be due to the variety of perspectives represented by each. One person interprets possible actions based on the effect they will have on people. Someone else is primarily concerned with profit. Another thinks about feasibility and scheduling. Others look at broad implications, practicality, or political consequences.

In the same way, children focus their conversations on whatever interests them, as long as the listener remains attentive. They will talk about that which is most meaningful to them and eagerly describe the activities, the sports, the play, the occasions, the projects, and the hobbies in which they can express themselves. Even though all children are involved in a variety of activities, each individual will repeatedly concentrate on certain things. You will eventually observe a consistency in what they like and dislike, and how they react in either case.

To encourage your child to tell his or her story and tell it in such a way as to be useful, keep the following suggestions in mind:

1. *Remember that your role is one of a listener.* All you should do is hear the story. This is not a matter of your child performing or trying to receive approval. It is simply an occasion in which you show interest in something that has happened.

2. *Ask questions to discover the facts of what he actually did.* A child's story telling skills are usually not well developed. Your questions will help the child fill in the missing parts. It is much like arranging the sequence of action in a movie so you can see the moves that have been made frame by frame. Sometimes a child will spend a long time telling a story, and other times less. Don't try to make a short story longer when there is no need to do so.

3. *Make sure your questions are only for clarification, because your child wants your approval.* He will be quick to change the plot of the story if he senses it will please you, or he will emphasize whatever he thinks you want to hear. You must be careful about manipulating his presentation. If you do not give any clues in this regard, he will proceed with the facts and, if given attention, stick to what he liked about doing what he did.

4. *The way children tell their stories is another indicator about how God designed them.* Some children are gifted with an interest in precision and detail. They will naturally supply you with stories rich in particulars. Other children will provide high points and not be inclined to share much more unless you indicate interest by asking specific questions. Children who someday will be known for their excellent skills in relating to people will display fragments of those gifts as they relate their stories specifically to you. Others whose gifts involve skills in working with things instead of people may not be eager to spend time on the stories except in social situations. So you may find it takes longer to get what you need in one case while receiving a wealth of material in another.

## LYLE'S STORY

Let's look at an example of a story-telling occasion by taking a look at Lyle. I will apply observation and story telling to see what I can discover of Lyle's true design. Here are some observations:

   • *Lyle plays a lot of football in front of*

*his house with neighborhood kids.*

* *Lyle's father is the coach. He's not outstanding as a coach, but Lyle still pays a lot of attention to him.*

* *The coach uses a lot of game plans scratched in the dust, more than you might expect for young kids in a neighborhood game.*

From your observations, you might come up with a number of possible conclusion—most of which are very much superficial at this point. You might be led to believe:

* *Lyle seems to love football since he plays so often.*
* *Lyle must be a great team player.*

* *Perhaps Lyle's dad is trying to give the young people a taste of what it is like to play football seriously.*

* *It seems that Lyle has the same devotion to football as his dad.*

At this point, it is time to encourage Lyle to do a little story telling. Remember that some people will require more prompting than others during this process.

"Hey, Lyle! What do you like to do with your time after school?"

*"I like to fish. Sometimes I build a fort in the woods. And sports."*

"What sports do you like?"

*"Well, I like fishing, like I said . . . and football . . . and tennis."*

"I've never seen you play tennis."

*"I play at school all the time. No one here plays tennis. I saw all the U.S. Open games on TV just before school began this year."*

"What about football?"

*"I play a lot of football."*

"At school?"

*"No. Just at home. My father gets up the games near our house. He loves football and coaches our team."*

"What do you like about football?"

*"I like playing with my father. He thinks I'm pretty good."*

"Are you pretty good?"

*"My father thinks so, so I guess I am!"*

"What else do you like about football?"

*"It keeps me in shape."*

"In shape for what?"

*"For tennis. You gotta run around a lot."*

"What do you like about tennis?"

*"Figuring out a way to beat the other guy. You gotta keep figuring out the way he does things and make sure you're ready for what he's gonna do next. It's fun when you guess right"*

"How about when you play football? Do you guess right then?"

*"It's hard because you can't keep track of everybody. But my father does."*

"How does he do that?"

*"I asked him to use those diagrams you see on the TV football games and in the movies. He knows how, and it shows me what I'm supposed to do in the game."*

"Is there anything you don't like about football?"

*"Yep! There are too many people to keep track of. But I like playing anyway, even though sometimes I get mad. Like sometimes I tackle a guy I don't like, just to get even."*

"You said that you like to fish. What do you like about it?"

*"I like going with my Dad."*

"What else do you like about it?"

*"Figuring out a way to get the fish by using the right lure. Somehow you've got to use the right fly at the right time. I know which ones to use, but I can't cast right."*

"So how do you get better at casting?"

"*I watch how my father does it and try to copy exactly what he does. I also have some books on fly fishing.*"

"Are the books helpful?"

"*Yes, I look at the pictures. They have draw-ings which show you how to hold the rod and the line, and how to cast. That helps, but it's hard to make it all work together. That's why I watch my father. It's easier when I can see it done.*"

"What do you like about fly-fishing?"

"*I like landing a fish even though it's hard to do. You have to know what you are doing, and if you do it right you have a fish. I like figuring out where the fish are biting and see what is hatching that they'll go for. I like getting the fly to act like the real thing and casting it to go where I think the fish are hiding.'*" What don't you like about fly-fishing?"

"*It takes so long to learn how to do it.*"

## INTERPRETING A CHILD'S STORIES

It is difficult to read the above dialogue and not see some consistencies within this single story.

For example, note Lyle's frequent use of "figured out". It is clear that figuring out things is a primary way for Lyle to learn.

And since he enjoys problem solving, his teachers would do well to approach almost all of his subjects from this perspective. The kind of problem solving he does, however, is strategic and involves beating an opponent (as noted in regard to his tennis matches and the fish). Providing some degree of head-to-head competition would enhance the situation for him. But it is not as if he wants to get a better grade than his competition. His strategy for winning focuses on the person with whom he is competing—figuring out his moves, his strengths, and his weaknesses.

If you were Lyle's English teacher, you might want to use the debate format with some degree of frequency (depending on Lyle's oral skills). Opportunities to go up against a classmate with similar competitive interests on a literary question would get both students involved in the appropriate literature. Lyle doesn't show a strong interest in reading as a way to learn in this story, so we do not know if he has a natural leaning toward literature. Even if not, this approach would probably pay off anyway. Certainly it would work better than trying to get him to study literature for its own sake.

Even though Lyle doesn't seem to be a reader, notice that he uses his visual capability with some degree of aggression. He wants his father to diagram the football plays so he can focus on one person at a time. He learns by seeing his dad demonstrate casting and from the illustrations in the books. Therefore, he will probably understand geometry better than algebra.

How does that fact help his English teacher? Actually, not a lot, but at least the teacher could recommend authors whose writing styles are full of imagery. Illustrated versions of books would encourage him if available. In teaching grammar, the old-fashioned method of diagraming sentences makes sense for students like Lyle. Similarly, time lines will help him understand the historical placement of different literary periods.

These suggestions would apply to Lyle regardless of his age. The way he prefers to learn is true of him as a first grader as well as a university graduate student. Your own experience should confirm this. We all learn in particular ways and have always learned that way. The way you were taught changed from class to class, but the way you actually assimilated the material was peculiar to who you were and are.

Lyle's stories bring up other interesting facts. Notice that the team situation was not particularly interesting to him. According to Lyle's own story, the team approach doesn't fit the way he prefers to work and play. Note also his strong interest in personal performance, especially in mastering specific techniques. As you can see, just these few items are invaluable when considering how to nurture Lyle in a way that fits who he is.

Remember not to reach any firm conclusions until you have gathered a lot of consistent information. The more important the decision to be made in a person's life, the greater degree of detailed evidence you want to gather.

Don't worry about whether or not consistency in someone's actions will be evident. It always is, if you know how to look.

## STORYTELLING AT VARIOUS AGES

Story telling can work for you in a couple of different ways. The first is when you ask about something you are observing or have seen previously. The child will give you some clues to what he liked about the activity and will better define your observations.

For instance, you see your son and daughter each creating some kind of structure with building blocks. You ask what they like about what they are doing. Your son says, "It looks like the firehouse down the street." Your daughter says, "It's something I made up myself."

Or perhaps you watch your nine year old and your sixteen year old each make a batch of cookies—an activity both of them enjoy. The younger child meticulously lays out all the utensils and lines up all the ingredients before he starts. He follows the recipe exactly, carefully measuring every item. You later ask what he enjoyed about making the cookies. He tells you that eating them was what he liked, and having the cookies turn out exactly the way he had planned. The sixteen year old, on the other hand, guesstimates his way through the whole project. He even throws in some almond extract that the recipe doesn't call for. When asked what he liked about the project, he is pleased that his creative efforts improved the taste of the cookies.

In both of these stories it is improper to

deem either child's behavior as more or less desirable than the other's. A child's actions and preferences are clear clues to his or her individual operating style. The fact that you throw your own cookie batter together haphazardly is no reason to think the nine year old has a rigid personality.

You can also see how a question or two can greatly enrich your understanding of your child's true feelings. This is good to know during the conversations about school that usually take place when children arrive at home.

If your child brings home an A on a test paper, you might want to find out what he likes about getting such a good grade. Perhaps it's because he worked so hard. Maybe he likes to surprise Mom and Dad. Or because it was the highest grade. Or because he likes to know when he's doing good work. Or because he got to clean the boards as a reward. Or that he doesn't really *like* to do the work, but feels he has to.

A second type of story telling is necessary when you didn't witness the child's accomplishment and are unable to make your own observations. In such instances you are more dependent on listening, but you can still record the important points in the child's narration of the event. Listening is an excellent way to spend quality time with your child because you are allowing him to share activities that mean the most to him. In addition you are learning more about this wonder, this person whom God has inserted into your family.

Your questions are still important to keep the narrative going and to enrich the detail of the story. You can't assume that everything the child did was likable. So at some point in the discussion, if the child isn't too young, be sure to find out what he did and didn't like about his activity.

## STORY TELLING BY YOUNG CHILDREN

Following are some examples of stories from a variety of ages. As you read them you will see how one child views the world much differently than another. First are a couple of conversations with a young child named Tommy.

### Tommy and His Schoolwork

"Hi, Tommy! What have you got there?"
*"Something I made in school."*

"Let's hang it up and look at it. I like all the colors. You glued things on it. That makes it look interesting."

*"You like it?"*

"Yes, I like it very much. I like looking at the work you do. Where did these colors come from?"

*"You know. That's paint."*

"Yes, I can see that you used paint, but I haven't seen a lot of these colors in a paint jar."

*"I mixed them."*

"How did you do that?"

*"I asked my teacher if I could. She gave me paper cups to use. She doesn't like mess."*

"How many colors did you mix?"

*"Lots. Some were no good. I washed them down the sink. I put some of the good ones in my drawing. I gave Billy some too. I like yellow, so I used a lot of it."*

"What do you like about yellow?"

*"You can make a lot of colors with yellow. I made green, orange, and brown.*

"That must have been fun. Where did you get the things to glue on your drawing?"

*"I found some of them. I did two drawings. My teacher had a box full of stuff . . . papers and things . . . and I used them in the first drawing.*

*In my other drawing I found things. See? Sticks . . . leaves . . . candy paper. I painted them."*

"Those things look fine in your drawing. Yes, you did a fine job. I like all the colors."

## Tommy and His Vacation

"Tell me, Tommy, what was your favorite thing on vacation?"

*"I liked the beach."*

"Yes. That is certainly a fun place. What did you like?"

*"I liked the sand and . . . I liked waves . . . and I liked the fort."*

"I liked the waves too. But I didn't see a fort."

*"I made one."*

"You did! Where did you make it?"

*"On the beach. I found things. I dug a hole with a stick and made it."*

"What did it look like?"

*"It had a roof and a flagpole. I put shells and stones in the wall. I pushed them into the sand."*

"Where did you get the flagpole?"

*"I found a long stick and made a flag by pushing a piece of paper on it. I made a road from the fort to the water. The waves kept messing it up. It was fun."*

## Conclusions about Tommy

I am not going to conclude from these two dialogues that Tommy is sure to become an artist or architect. At this point he is merely exercising some basic motor and expressive skills.

But we should certainly take note of his interest in experimenting on his own. He doesn't seem to need more than a rough idea of how to do something. He will then experiment somewhat independently, using available materials to which he is attracted. In these two stories the objects he uses are natural—leaves, sticks, shells, stones. This may be coincidental, but we should look to see if he is drawn to similar objects in future stories.

Here are some additional tentative conclusions that can't be determined for sure (yet). But if additional stories provide further confirmation, we can be fairly sure of the validity of this evidence.

1. Tommy seems to work quite independently of others in work and play. He needs an environment where he can operate in solo roles with some degree of

frequency. Yet he may also need occasional encouragement to get involved with some kind of study/athletic/project team. Family get-togethers are another place where he can be urged to participate in a group. But he should be praised regularly for his ability to do things on his own.

2. So far Tommy apparently likes closure and probably would not thrive on being taken from one project and placed on another before the first was finished. If this holds up in future observations or stories, he should be given chores which don't require a long time to finish. Smaller projects, assigned one at a time, will be more geared to his design.

3. Speaking of chores, don't be surprised if Tommy modifies them somewhat so he can experiment a bit. As long as he gets the main task accomplished, he might do well to complete some of the smaller jobs in his own way. But if he modifies the task so completely that he really is not doing what he should, he needs to be gently challenged to focus his attention

on the important things, while recognizing his natural inclinations.

4. Tommy will be greatly affirmed if you ask for his opinion occasionally. You might check with him to see where he would put some plants in the garden or how he would arrange the tools hanging in the garage. And as he builds confidence in himself, you will recognize that he has a contribution to make and particular abilities to be noted.

5. When Tommy is learning something, leave room for him to make mistakes. Since he's an experimenter, he's going to try some things that won't work out. Generally, he should be given praise for getting the right results without worrying that he may have done some extra tinkering to get there.

6. Tommy doesn't need a lot of plastic toys to entertain himself. For him, the best toys are things that can be used to make other things. And if the evidence continues to support this supposition, he should be given a workplace somewhere

in the house. He should be encouraged to accumulate whatever materials and tools that make sense to him. In fact, the pattern of tools he gathers through the years may be the best display of his interests.

7. One of the best things Tommy's parents can do is to provide lots of opportunities for him to see and experience various situations and environments. After they provide him with several options, they can see in which direction he is drawn. Then they can act on their observations.

## STORY TELLING BY ELEMENTARY SCHOOL CHILDREN

Many of these things that are true of Tommy would be very frustrating to Kathleen, an elementary school student.

### Kathleen's School Assignment

"Kathleen, I heard you got an excellent grade for a history project. Congratulations on a good job. What kind of project was it?"

*"I wrote a ten-page paper about the thirteen Colonies. I also made a map as big as a poster*

*for when I read the paper."*

"That is a pretty big project. Did you like doing it?"

*"I loved writing the paper best and I also liked doing the map."*

"Tell me about writing the paper."

*"I had to do it for my social studies class. My teacher gave us a list of subjects we could write about. We had to do one of them."*

"And you picked the Colonies."

*"It was the first one on the list, so I wrote about that."*

"What did you do first?"

*"I asked my teacher how long it should be. She told me about ten pages. She also gave me a book on the Colonies to get me started."*

"Then what?"

*"The next day she taught us how to do a research paper and wrote the steps on the board. I copied it down and then figured how long I should spend on each step. I had two weeks to finish it. I made out a schedule and each day I would do the work for that day. I wanted to get it done a day early in case anything happened."*

"What kinds of things did you have to do?"

*"I had to read a bunch of books, take notes, and line up the notes in order. Then I had to*

write a one-page outline. Then I had to write the paper."

"What parts did you like to do?"

"I liked all of it, but the reading was hard. I like reading but I didn't have time to read it all. I had to skip over things. I didn't want to, because the books were interesting."

"Did you know what books to read?"

"I went to the librarian at my school. My teacher said she gave her a list of the subjects we could write on. She showed me how to find the books, but I couldn't take them all home in case anyone else was going to write on the same subject. I could take two at a time. Writing the notes was hard—real hard because I was writing too much. I was going to have more notes than I could use in the paper! But my father showed me how to pick the important parts."

"Then what?"

"Then I made piles of notes according to the topic— farming . . . shipping . . . like that. Then I put them in order."

"How did you know what order to put them in?"

"I looked at the table of contents in one of the books and used that order—though I didn't have as many topics. That made it easy to write the paper. I just took the first pile of notes and wrote a couple of paragraphs and kept on going through all the piles. I ended with twelve pages and my father helped me cut it down to ten."

"What about the map?"

"We had to read our papers in front of the class and I thought it would be easier for the class if I had a map to point to when I read. In the school I used to go to, my teacher had a big map of the thirteen Colonies which she could pull down when she was teaching. I made my own, but I couldn't pull it down—it was like a poster. My mother helped me with that part. She likes art things. She showed me how to use a grid to enlarge the map out of the book. You make small squares on the small map and then you make the same number of squares on the poster board only they are much bigger. Then you draw in the large square what's in the small square and then you connect it all and then you've got a big map. It was hard but kinda fun."

"Well, we know what you liked in this project. Was there anything you didn't like?"

"Yes. I didn't like reading in front of the class. It turned out OK, but I don't like doing that."

This is only one of Kathleen's stories. You would normally want to accumulate a

number of them in order to come to the
conclusions I present here, but this story is
a good example of how she operates.
Instead of presenting a number of conclusions as I did with Tommy, let's focus on
one very important item.

## Conclusions about Kathleen

It should be apparent that Kathleen likes to
avoid confusion. The very first thing she did
in regard to this assignment was to select
the first topic on the list. Then she proceed-
ed to ask the teacher for some direction. If
no one provides the desired specifications,
she starts asking questions and probing
until she is provided with what she needs.
Once the requirements are in place, she
loves delivering what is expected.

If Kathleen's operating style isn't identi-
fied, she may undergo some very confusing
times. She will be an outstanding performer
for teachers who have a structured syllabus,
exact goals, and clear expectations in their
assignments. But teachers who have an
open-ended approach to a subject, ask for
opinions, and expect independent choices in
projects will wonder why she "doesn't
show initiative." Kathleen's parents need to

be aware of this situation so that a very bright girl doesn't come to the conclusion that she really isn't too smart.

Kathleen doesn't need to be told how to make every move, but she does need to know two things: what is expected of her, and how to use the tools to get there. Once the goals are set, she is quite able to do whatever is necessary to achieve them. And if this one chunk of understanding was all Kathleen's parents got out of going through this whole exercise, they would have enough information to help her avoid self-doubt, confusion, and hurt. They could show her that not all intelligent children operate in the same way.

## STORY TELLING BY OLDER CHILDREN

Older children can reflect on activities of early childhood as well as recent events in significant detail. They can provide extensive histories rich with activities, play, people, happenings, and other things they liked. The listener is placed in a position of observing the meaningful part of the storyteller's daily living. Such memories stay vivid in the storytellers' minds because they are expressive of whom God made them to be. Take, for example, the 45-year-old man who could recall the time he learned to unlock the gate of his playpen as a child. Amazing! Even a person who treats last month as ancient history can still find a bounty of truly meaningful memories stored in his or her cranium.

## Mark and His Summer Job

Let's now listen to Mark, a high schooler recall a project he really liked.

*"About a year ago I decided that I needed to earn more money during the summer than I could from just mowing lawns, like I had been doing since Middle School. I spent some time thinking about what I could do just for the summer. Then I thought about growing things, so I went to see a truck farmer about a mile down the road who set up a large roadside stand every year. I asked him if there was anything he wasn't planning to grow that I could supply him with, or anything he wasn't able to grow enough of. He was interested in having me supply several vegetables if I was interested. But he needed lots of each item, and though I lived on a farm I hadn't ever been responsible for a whole crop. So I went to my father and asked if it was possible for me plow anything he wasn't using. My father said it*

was OK with him, but that I would need help and he couldn't afford the time."

"So, what did you do?"

"I asked a friend of mine if he was interested in helping me. We made a deal where if the project was a success, he would share in the profits, and if for some reason it failed I wouldn't have to pay him. He had helped me build up the lawn-mowing business, so I think he thought we would be a success for sure. He had to get up early in the morning to work with me, which he hated. But he worked hard. I knew he would."

"Did you know what to do in raising the crops?"

"Not really. Our farm was mostly dairy. Oh, I had helped my mom with her garden every summer—plowing and weeding mostly—but that was nothing compared to what I had to do now. So I asked the guy I was going to sell the crops to if he could give me some pointers after I got the land plowed. He gave me lots of good advice about how early to plant and repeat crops and stuff like that. Then I got some more pointers from the county agent especially about how to keep the insect population down. He also told me what fertilizers to use and how to stagger the planting so everything didn't come in at once. He was real smart about that stuff. So all

*that summer me and my friend worked like*
*slaves—him more than me because I packed the*
*truck and took the stuff to the farmer's stand*
*each day and kept track of how much we were*
*making. But my friend and I both made a lot of*
*money that summer. The farmer's stand was on*
*a busy highway and near a lot of vacation*
*homes, so he had lots of business and bought*
*almost everything we delivered."*

Mark's story was presented pretty much
as he told it, but I could have gotten a better
understanding of him by asking a few questions. I can tell that Mark tends to engage
individuals as a resource, and if this habit is
repeated in his other stories, then we are on
to something. Yet we also need to get an
understanding about his approach to other
people. The question, "What did you say to
him?" would have been useful. What kind
of conversations did he have with the truck
farmer, his father, his friend, and the county
agent?

Mark says, "All that summer me and my
friend worked like slaves." What exactly did
Mark do? What tasks did his friend do?
What does it mean to him to "work like a
slave"? When he says he packed the truck,
we might assume we know what that means

because we have packed trucks ourselves. But perhaps Mark packs a truck in a truly unique way. Think about your own experience: one person will carefully plan how to fit things on a truck, another will figure it out while doing it, and still another will pile things in it without any thought. So having Mark tell you about packing the truck may prove useful—not by itself, but in connection with later information about how he organizes his room, packs his luggage for a trip, handles his homework assignments, and structures his research for term papers.

We could also ask about all the tasks he mentions. If we discover that he was involved in the weeding, we would ask him to tell us those details.

*"Weeding? Why, I did that the same every day. I would get there about seven in the morning while it was still cool. I would use only two tools: a hand rake which I hung off my belt for whenever I needed to use it on some big clump of weeds growing right in the bed, and the hoe. I divided the rows up so that between me and my friend, we would have the whole field completely hoed in five days. When you do it that way and stay on top of it, all you have to do is chop young weeds into the ground. I like*

*staying on top of it all. It's great to see it all neat
and orderly, with all the rows straight and not a
weed to be seen. All that summer, every time I
drove past the field I loved looking at it. Funny,
you'd think I'd be tired of seeing it with all the
sweat I poured into it, but I wasn't."*

From Mark's description of weeding the
field, you could probably predict the answers
to how he would pack the truck or do his
homework. You can't know for sure without
more evidence, but you wouldn't be surprised to discover you were right.

## EVALUATING DISLIKE

Whenever you question a storyteller about
what he has told you, it is usually helpful to
have him identify anything he disliked about
the activity. Often certain requirements of an
activity need to be satisfied, but are not
enjoyed by the storyteller. We shouldn't
assume that he liked everything he did until
after we've asked, "Was there anything you
didn't like about this activity?"

Just as there is consistency in what we
like to do, there is also consistency in what
we don't like to do. When strong themes of
both extremes are evident, they usually
function as contrasts to provide a picture of

the individual's operating style that is vivid with color. What we don't want to do is perceive these dislikes as weaknesses.

A common practice in corporate settings is to evaluate managers and then try to develop them by improving on their weaknesses rather than investing in their strengths. Yet no amount of training will transform a person with marginal analytical abilities into a brilliant analyst. You may not be able to sing like Luciano Pavarotti, but in no way should that be considered a weakness. Nor is there reason to believe you could ever be trained to accomplish his level of talent. And just as you might never be known for your singing, other people are never going to be creative geniuses, analytical experts, corporate managers, or entrepreneurial wizards. But the lack of a specific gift should not be labeled a "weakness."

So would it be wrong to provide training that will improve performance in an area which is not a strength? Of course not. Sharpening some basic skills can make sense as long as we don't push too hard on someone without the right gifts. If a child is not a gifted writer, he still needs to develop a certain level of writing skills as a basic tool in life. We would do well, however, not to spend time and resources attempting to match his writing skills to those things for which he is really gifted. Equal performance in all areas of study and activity is not a logical standard of an educational program.

As we consider the dislikes of children, we should remember that some are merely cultural, others are a matter of personal taste, and still others are seriously a matter of contrast—the opposites of what they are gifted to do. We know that to train a child in an area of strength will have a rich payoff, equipping the child to do that which he or she is gifted to do. On the other hand, some tasks do not align at all with the child's design.

We can discard the model of an excellent child being one who does all things well, or who is at least working on it. Rather, your child will achieve excellence as he or she discovers (with your help) the individual design that God has bestowed, and eventually learns how that design can produce results that no one else can duplicate.

# HELPING FAMILIES GROW SERIES

❧ *Communicating Spiritual Values Through Christian Music*

❧ *Equipping Your Child for Spiritual Warfare*

❧ *Family Vacations That Work*

❧ *Helping Your Child Stand Up to Peer Pressure*

❧ *How to Discover Your Child's Unique Gifts*

❧ *How to Work With Your Child's Teachers*

❧ *Helping Your Child Love to Read*

❧ *Improving Your Child's Self-Image*

❧ *Preparing for Your New Baby*

❧ *Should My Child Listen to Rock Music?*

❧ *Spiritual Growth Begins at Home*

❧ *Surviving the Terrible Teenage Years*

# ABOUT THE AUTHOR

Ralph Mattson is the president of The Doma Group in Minneapolis and a management and human resource consultant to corporations. He has much experience in keying into people's strengths and helping them manage those strengths. His additional experience as Headmaster for 9 1/2 years and father of four have provided a good base for understanding children.

Mr. Mattson has written four books, including *Discovering Your Child's Design*. He lives with his wife in Canton Center, Connecticut.